AMP

ASIAN MALE PORTRAITS

1

2011-2015

WEST PHILLIPS

Behind the scenes:
Josh
Seoul, South Korea
2014

I began photography as a hobby rather unexpectedly in the fall of 2009 while living in New York City. I had never taken any sort of photography class, but found this growing inspiration in the environment around me and wanted to capture it as best I could. I had a new camera, some really vague ideas and absolutely no direction. I knew I wanted to photograph the people in my life at the time, so my first few subjects were people I had close relationships with and who inspired me in one way or another.

In the spring of 2010 I moved to San Francisco - what I consider to really be the starting point of my photography career. While working my office job, I used my free time to seek out new subjects for my budding art. I can remember how awkward and insecure I felt at the beginning, having to convince (beg) people to let me photograph them. I felt the brunt of rejection more times than I care to admit! The more photoshoots I did, the more confident I became and this newfound passion grew stronger with each one.

I noticed from the very beginning a clear lack of Asian male models in western media. My early interest in photographing Asian males wasn't to make any sort of statement, but rather to capture an image and look I found appealing. As my work and experience grew, so did my exposure. While most of the comments and feedback I received were encouraging and supportive, I was shocked by the number of people who would blatantly tell me my photos would be better if the models weren't Asian. It was these negative comments that I have to thank for putting me and my art on the path it is today.

This volume serves as a retrospective - a chronological collection of some of my earlier work from 2011 - 15. Spanning several countries, the models in the following pages represent not only my growing and changing art, but also a personal glimpse into where I've been and where I'm going. Through close friends, acquaintances, professional relationships as well as more intimate relationships, I hope that these selected photos do justice to some of the incredible people I've been fortunate enough to know and work with. Without them, none of this would be possible.

West Phillips

first met Peter Le in 2011, while we were both living in San Francisco. I had only been doing photography for a year or so at that point and Peter was one of my first clients. After working together on some photo and video projects, we became fast friends. Since then, we've collaborated on many shoots together, around the U.S. and also in China.

Doyle
Northern California, USA
2011

Hank
Northern California, USA
2011

Leo
Sydney, Australia
2011

Rick
Sydney, Australia
2011

Andy
San Diego, USA
2012

Ethan
San Diego, USA
2012

Don
Virginia, USA
2012

Shu
Beijing, China
2013

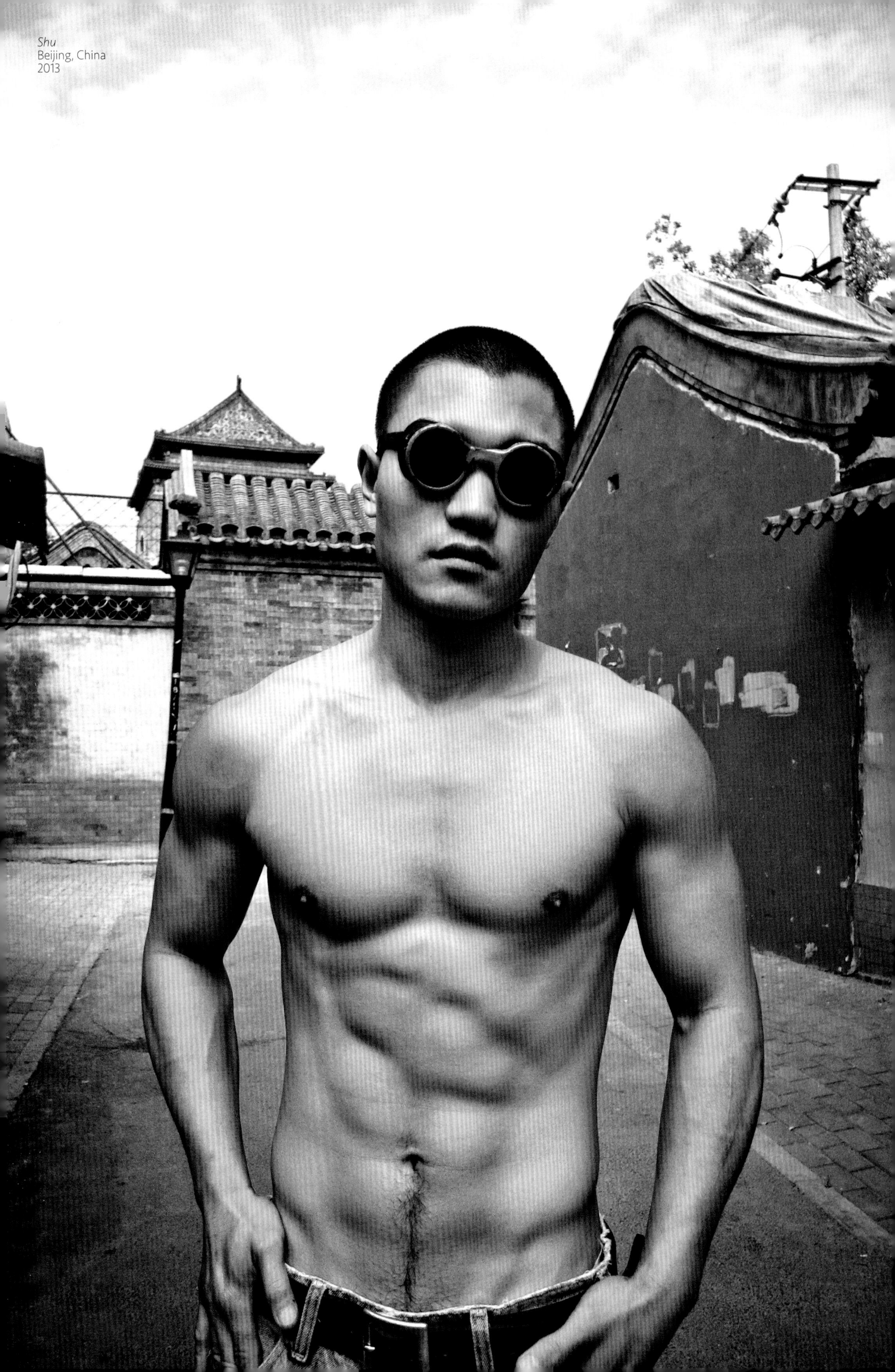

Shu
Beijing, China
2013

I began the *Underworld* series soon after I arrived in China. With the seemingly constant high pollution levels, I had the idea to incorporate gas masks as props into some of the more sexy and raw shoots that I was doing. It soon became not just a message for environmental issues, but social issues as well.

Leo
Beijing, China
2013

Peter
Beijing, China
2013

Jacky
Malaysia
2013

James
Malaysia
2013

Daniel
Malaysia
2013

請勿停

早上5點至晚上8點

請勿停
敬請合作

Em
Bangkok, Thailand
2013

Brian
Bangkok, Thailand
2013

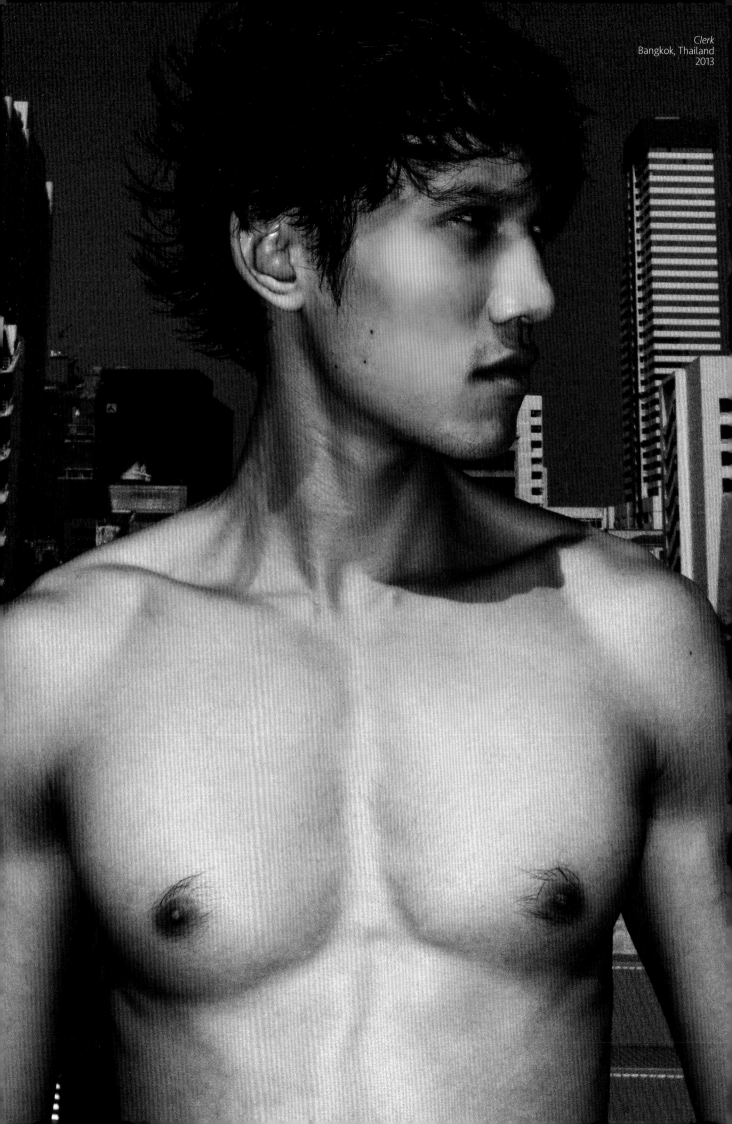

Kingley
Bangkok, Thailand
2013

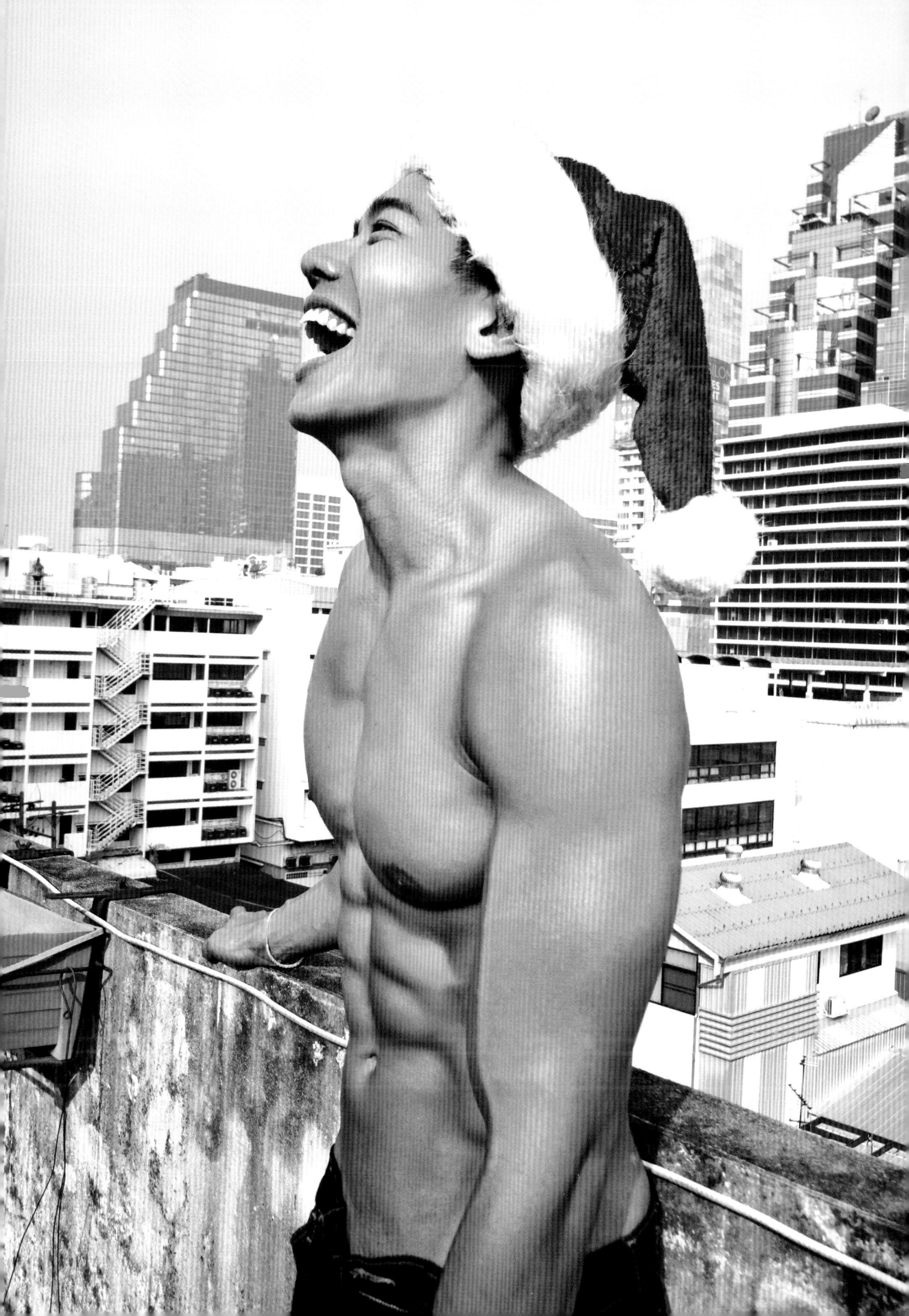

Jason
Singapore
2013

Randy
Miami Beach, USA
2014

Shuichi
Miami Beach, USA
2014

Young
Beijing, China
2014

Libra
Beijing, China
2014

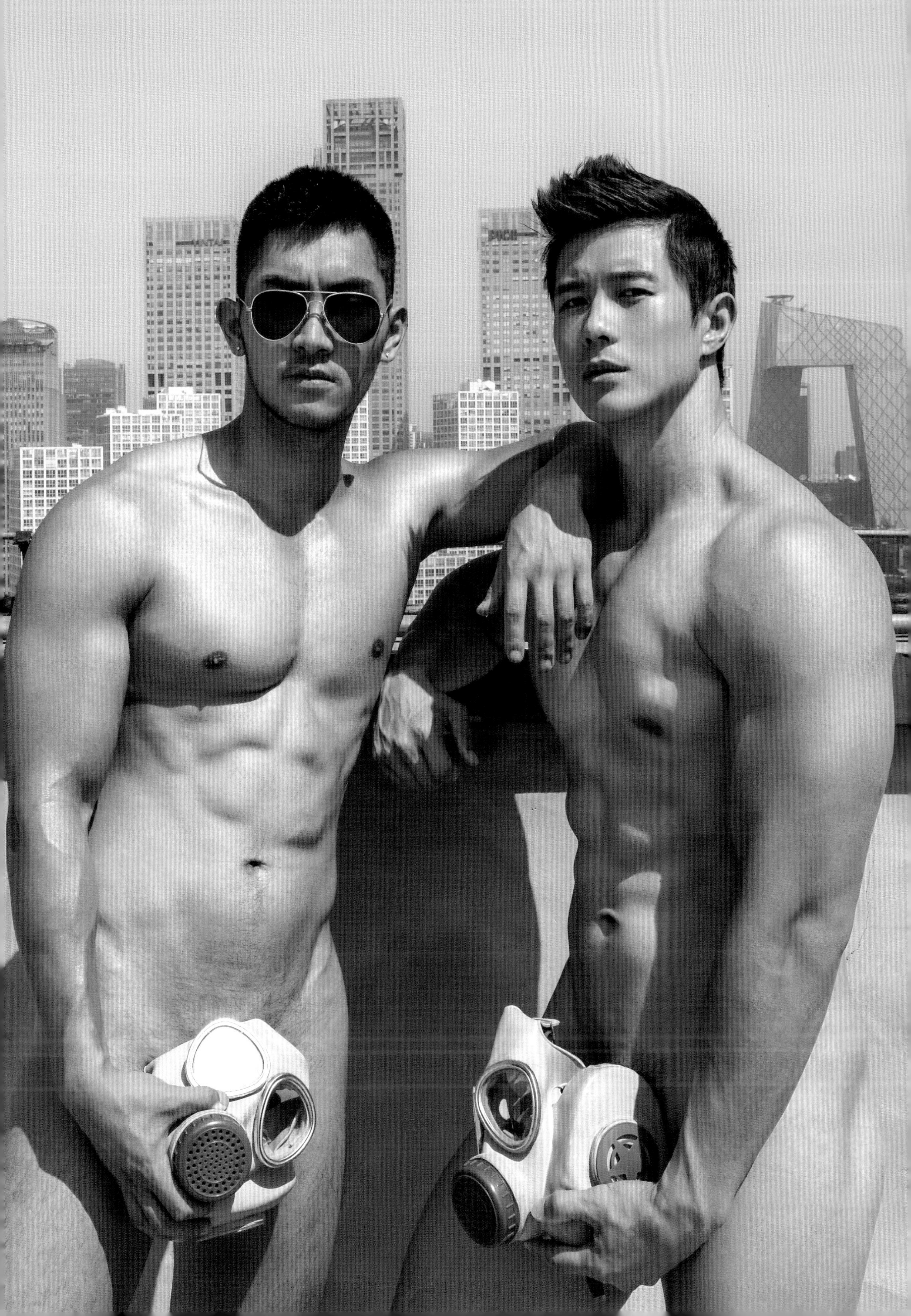

Peter & Eric
Beijing, China
2014

Josh
Seoul, S. Korea
2014

Yunqi
Beijing, China
2015

Luk Luk
Beijing, China
2015

Nemo
Beijing, China
2015

Aiden
Seoul, S. Korea
2015

Sean
Beijing, China
2015

Paul & XiaoChen
Beijing, China
2015

Wangjie
Beijing, China
2015

Jon
Los Angeles, USA
2015

Behind the scenes:
Kevin & Libra
Beijing, China
2015

AMP
Copyright © 2018 West Phillips
westphillips.com

Design and layout by Johnny Lu Studio
johnny-lu.com

ISBN 978-1-7320888-1-8

Printed and bound in China.

in partnership with

IMPERIAL COMMERCE LTD

imperialcommerce.co.uk